The Official

Cat Codependents Handbook

The Official
Cat Codependents
Handbook

For People Who Love Their Cats
Too Much

by

Ronnie Sellers

Illustrated by Jennifer Black Reinhardt

Published by Ronnie Sellers Productions

Library of Congress Catalog Card Number: 95-092292
ISBN # 1-56906-019-3

Book design by Darci Mehall, Aureo Design

Ronnie Sellers Productions makes books available at special discounts when purchased in bulk for special sales promotions, premiums, fund raising or educational use. Special books, or book excerpts, can also be created to fit specific needs. For details, contact our sales department at 1-800-MAKE-FUN (625-3386).

RONNIE SELLERS PRODUCTIONS
P. O. BOX 71
KENNEBUNK, ME 04043

Manufactured in the United States of America

First printing July 1995
10 9 8 7 6 5 4 3 2 1

Acknowledgements

The author would like to acknowledge the following for the contributions they made to the publication of this book . . .

Tigger

Euripides

Boris

Chezzie

Melvin

Melinda

Ariel

Dedications

This book is fondly dedicated to those of you who have written me
to confess the many different ways you love your cats too much.

Ronnie Sellers

❧

To my great loves, Joe and Eliza. And to my terrific family.
Thank you.

Jennifer Black Reinhardt

Author's Note

Four years ago the first edition of The Official Cat Codependents Calendar was published. On the back page of that calendar and in subsequent editions, I invited people to write to *Cat Codependents Anonymous* care of our editorial office to tell us *their cat stories*.

Since then I have collected thousands of letters. The letters come from people from all walks of life: school teachers, lawyers, housewives, psychologists, veterinarians, children. Some of the letters are only one paragraph long; others go on for ten pages. Most of them are intended to be funny, but often I wonder whether I should be laughing in response to what I'm reading...or crying.

The letters have one thing in common. They are all written by people who love their cats *very* much.

I have included some of these letters, or excerpts from them, in this book to help illustrate the various aspects of cat codependency. These testimonials corroborate my observations about Cat Codependents and prove that they are not merely figments of my imagination.

I promised the authors of these letters that I would respect their privacy. I have, therefore, included only their initials and their home towns with their letters. If you think you recognize someone whose letter is included here, please don't phone or write me for verification. I am sworn to secrecy on the life of my mother's pet persian.

And if you do recognize respondents, *please don't use their admissions about their cat codependence against them.* After all, it seems that most of us are addicted to something these days. One could do a lot worse than to choose a cat.

🐾

❧

Table of Contents

Introduction xi

Chapter One: Symptoms of Cat Codependency...2

Chapter Two: The Causes of Cat Codependency...22

Chapter Three: When Someone You Love Loves Cats...40

Chapter Four: Financial Consequences of Cat Codependency..................................58

Chapter Five: Cat Codependent Families...76

Chapter Six: Coping with Cat Codependence 94

Afterword 112

Introduction

I was visiting a book store in New England one lovely August afternoon to autograph copies of one of the children's books I authored. The bookseller seated me at a small table in the middle of the self improvement section. The irony of this was not lost on me. I had been going to marriage counselling for almost twelve months by then, making what proved to be a futile attempt to save my marriage. During that time I had read many of the books that I was now surrounded by.

The turnout was good. I signed more than fifty books before the end of the first hour. Then a woman approached me and asked if she could purchase twelve autographed books. I turned to the bookseller. He nodded, indicating that he had sufficient supply to accommodate her. "Sure," I said congenially. "Who is the first book for?"

"Tinkerbelle," was her response.

"Okay," I said, and I signed a book for Tinkerbelle, assuming that this was a nickname for one of her grandchildren. "And the next book?" I asked.

"Muffy," she replied. "Actually, could you sign it to "Fluffy Muffy?"

"Certainly," I said. I autographed Fluffy Muffy's book while secretly wondering how anyone could burden an innocent child with such a nickname. "And the next?"

"Felix," she said gleefully. "Felix loves picture books more than any of the others."

I became suspicious. When she asked for books for Tigger and Fussy, Manxie and Gussy, my curiosity got the better of me.

"Excuse me, Ma'am," I said, "if you don't mind my saying so, these all sound like cat names."

"Of course they do," she said with an explosive laugh, "that's because they are!" and she slapped me on the arm with such force that I was knocked into the Leo Buscaglia section.

"You buy children's books for your cats?" I asked guardedly as I pulled myself back up into my chair.

"Not exclusively," she replied. "Max likes art books...Gaugin in particular. Boris favors Gary Larsen."

"How many cats do you own?"

"I don't own any of them. Quite the contrary, in fact. They own me."

"Alright then," I persisted, "how many cats own you?"

She bent down over my table and looked directly into my eyes. "Guess," she said intently.

I looked at the list of cat names she was holding. "Twelve?" It seemed like a reasonable guess.

She was silent. Her eyes grew wider as she allowed the tension to build. "Wrong!" she bellowed as she whacked me on the other shoulder and sent me flying into the John Bradshaw shelf. "I have thirteen. But Hugo hates books."

With that she nearly became hysterical, laughing uproariously as she hoisted me up off of the floor, plopped me down into my chair again and shoved the pen back into my hand.

For the next ninety minutes Loretta, as I learned she was called, regaled me with one story after another about her cats while I autographed books for the other patrons of the store.

I learned that she had story hour for her "babies" every evening at 7 pm, at which time all of her cats (except Hugo) cuddled up with her in her armchair near the fireplace. The cats, Loretta explained, stared at the illustrations while she read the text out loud and turned the pages of that evening's featured picture book.

I learned in great detail about each of her cat's idiosyncrasies; which ones liked canned food, which ones ate only freshly caught fish, which ones were vegetarians, which ones were catnip addicts and what they did while under the influence.

Then, very suddenly, Loretta fell silent.

"What time is it?" she asked anxiously.

"It's about ten minutes before six o'clock," I told her.

"Oh no!" she exclaimed as she scooped up her armful of autographed books and plopped some money onto the table. "I've got to leave *right* now. I've got to turn on Wheel of Fortune for Tigger at 6 pm or he'll be furious! Goodbye and thanks."

Loretta was gone before I even had a chance to reply. I signed a few more books for the last customers and then sat there alone among all of the self improvement books.

I pulled out my note pad and jotted down the words "Cat Codependents: People Who Love Their Cats Too Much."

After meeting Loretta, I began to notice that there were many others like her whose lives seemed to revolve around their relationships with their cats. I began to record my observations about these "cat codependent" people whenever I encountered one. I learned quickly that there was no shortage of subject matter.

After a few months of taking notes, I sent some of my observations and ideas about how they could be illustrated to Jennifer Black Reinhardt, a wonderfully gifted illustrator (and *true cat codependent*) whom I had worked with previously. The next morning there were five or six hilarious sketches from Jennifer waiting for me in my fax machine. Those sketches became the basis for *The Official Cat Codependents Calendar*, published later that year. The calendar was an immediate success.

Jennifer and I had no idea what we had tapped into back then. Even now, after four years and more than a quarter of a million calendars sold, we're still not sure what to make of it.

One thing is for certain, though; tomorrow morning I will go out and open my mailbox and there will be letters in it from Cat Codependents from all over the world. The letters will be warm and funny and will contain stories about things the authors have done for the love of their cats. They will lift my spirits as I read them over my morning coffee. They will remind me again that we are, by and large, compassionate, caring creatures who need to give love and affection as much as we need to receive it. Our pets offer us the opportunity to nurture and to care for other living beings *unconditionally*. They make us feel needed. Feeling needed makes us feel more alive.

The letters always leave me feeling hopeful and good...and grateful for having received them.

Loretta, wherever you are, I am forever in your debt.

The Official
Cat Codependents
Handbook

Chapter 1
Symptoms of Cat Codependency

...Boo will be 18 in February. I buy her food & litter before I buy my own groceries. I've had three other cats since that fateful day in 1980 when Boo CHOSE ME as her new owner. I have loved each one more than I ever thought possible.

They're not just a comfort...they're my best friends.

D.K.
OKC, OK

A Cat Codependent's first thought in the morning is about the cat.

Cat Codependents are often the last to realize that they are powerless and their lives have become unmanageable.

Hi Cat Lovers,

I have 20 or more cats. I have to sleep on my couch and I never have any room.

I have a button that says "The more people I meet, the more I love my cats."

Thank You

E.T.
Edmonton, Alberta
Canada

Cat Codependents love nothing more than 'flashing' photos of their pets.

Dear Cat Codependents,

The truth is out!

I work with a wide variety of people as a librarian at the Seattle Public Library and I have encountered many fellow Cat Codependents during the course of reference interactions that have to do with cats.

I've often gone so far as to show my cat photos to virtual strangers, library patrons who adore cats, as well as friends and colleagues.

Many Meows,

L.A.
Seattle, WA

As might be expected, multiple cat ownership is almost always a sign of Cat Codependency. In fact, serious Cat Codependents have a motto: If you know how many cats you have, you don't have enough.

Cat Codependents Anonymous

Thank You! Finally someone has recognized the need for an organization such as yours. I now know I am not alone in this illness.

Please put me on your (future) mailing lists.

I currently own somewhere between five and ten cats (depending upon what type of food I happen to be serving).

Cat Codependent Forever,

RECEIVED 4/20

C.B.
McKeesport, PA

Privacy is one of the first things a Cat Codependent learns to live without.

BLACK

Cat Codependents drop everything the moment their cats need their attention.

Hi!

Friends & co-workers always ask me for help in finding wayward cats new homes. I often pay for the homeless to get their shots and also medical care.

This past year my "babies" all had their cavities filled and Baby (my youngest) now loves to have her teeth brushed. Virginia (my best friend ever) has been dieting and recently received The Healthy Cat Award at her vet's.

Do I sound like the proud parent? Yes, I am becoming slightly more eccentric with each new cat. I have a feeling that it will slowly catch me. Someday I will wake up to cats everywhere! I am already known as 'Cat Woman.'

I am hopelessly addicted; add me to your mailing list!

Sincerely,

N.E.W.
Exton, PA

Cat Codependents will only patronize "cat friendly" resorts. After all, what fun would a holiday be without the cats? And besides, leaving them behind in some sort of kitty compound would be out of the question. The poor things might be emotionally scarred for life by the experience.

A fringe group of Cat Codependents in California believe that their cats are famous people reincarnated.

Einstein

Van Gogh

ELVIS

Cyrano

Marilyn

BLACK

Every Cat Codependent knows that the way to a cat's heart is through its stomach.

Cat Codependents,

I am as Cat Codependent as you can get. My cats come first always! When I was first starting my business I was really broke. My cats ate before I did. And they always got their normal food, never cheap or generic.

One of my cats only likes 'human' tuna fish, so of course that's what she gets. Molly Jean will only eat very fresh crunchies - once they get even the slightest bit stale I have to dump them. Chelsea Ann loves evaporated milk with her meals. Buddy hasn't gotten finicky yet, but he will.

People think my cats are spoiled, but I don't believe you can spoil a cat too much. They give me tons of unconditional love.

My cats are my life,

C.M.
Tucson, AZ

Chapter 2
The Causes of Cat Codependency

Dear Folks,

I really think you should investigate the hereditary nature of Cat Codependency. I am quite sure there is a gene somewhere for it. I had very little chance of not becoming a Cat Codependent. Both my mother and father were cat lovers. I have pictures of me as a baby in a playpen with cats all around, staying just far enough away so that I couldn't reach them, of course. When I grew up and got out on my own I went by the "one cat per household" rule for many years and kept my addiction under control. However, when I lost the greatest cat ever, my beautiful calico Margaret, things began to fall apart. It probably didn't help any that I started volunteering at the local cat shelter...sort of like an alcoholic working at a bar.

I started adding cats at the rate of about one every six months. I now have five cats. As you can see, I am a victim of Cat Codependency. I am almost 50 and just want to have more cats. It is all my parents' fault and I thank them for it every time I see one of my cats or hear their purrs or stroke their beautiful fur. Without them my life would be much sadder and infinitely lonely. They ask so little and give so much.

Yours,

C.B.
Binghamton, NY

RECEIVED
2/12

While there is little data to support the theory, many Cat Codependents believe their condition is hereditary...that there is some cat gene they inherited from their ancestors and will pass on to their children and grandchildren.

Dear Cat Codependents Anonymous,

I am very glad to say that I inherited my Cat Codependency from my dearly departed grandmother. She actually fed every cat in the neighborhood, had cats all over her back yard and always had a box of kittens under her bed.

At this writing I have 8 cats living with me. I feel very blessed that God picked my grandmother and me to help love his little kittens.

K.L.
Fort Worth, TX

RECEIVED
1/12

A different school contends that Cat Codependency is a strain of a highly contagious virus that spreads easily wherever people congregate.

Still others believe they have a kind of natural "cat magnetism" which causes them to attract needy, helpless cats the way some people attract lint.

Dear Folks,

My family has always loved cats, but we didn't become cat codependent until a couple of years ago after the tragic death of Joe, our beloved cat companion of eight years.

After Joe departed, our house became what I have often called a "cat magnet." The height of our cat codependence came last summer when we had, for a while, a grand total of ten kitties.

Though we enjoy this affliction, we need all the help we can get.

G.B.
Lake City, AR

Cat codependent men tend to attribute their Cat Codependence to "a chance meeting with destiny."

Freudians believe that Cat Codependency stems from an unresolved conflict with a cat during childhood.

Dear Cat Codependents Anonymous,

My cat codependence started when I was eight.
Now, 40 years later, it's in "control" due to space limitations. Molly & Emily share their apartment with me.

It began when I started taking care of an occasional stray cat or two. Word spread. One evening when my father came home he took a look at my "babies" - on the fence, patio, window ledges, in the utility room. There were 26!

"Where are all these damn cats coming from?" he bellowed. My response was "I don't know, Daddy. I'm just feeding them."

I think he too may have been a Cat Codependent...thereafter my allowance always included enough for cat food.

Sincerely,

RECEIVED
5/14

V.D.
Mobile, Alabama

The ancients believed that Cat Codependency was "karma" for having treated cats disrespectfully in a previous life.

Medieval folklore warned that pregnant women who let purring cats rest on their laps bear children who love Muffin more than Mama.

Cat Codependency can strike suddenly and when least expected. Mary and George agreed to take care of their neighbor's very portly cat while she went "to the city to do a little shopping." What the neighbor failed to tell them was that the cat was pregnant and the city she was going to was Bangkok. The next morning Mary and George found themselves taking care of seven cats. They are still waiting for their neighbor to return from Bangkok.

Why do I love them so much? All 21 of them. Yes, I said 21. This is what happens when you catch two strays who both turn out to be very pregnant and give birth to 10 offspring. I already had 11 cats that I was trying to explain to myself, then "Oh look, aren't those kitties cute?" They would be a lot cuter if they weren't ALL MINE, but I can't seem to get rid of this incurable disease of loving the little critters.

21 used to be my lucky number.

RECEIVED 9/17

M.S.
Paso Robles, CA

Chapter 3

When Someone You Love Loves Cats

Hello,

My husband and I are owned by 3 neutered male indoor-only cats (they also control my Great Dane!). I don't think my husband ever imagined what he was getting into when he married me four years ago (back when it was only two cats).

All in all, my husband is pretty good natured about it (he was not a cat person before). I've received the usual cat jewelry, socks and calendars and he doesn't grumble too loudly when our bed is crowded with warm furballs who are looking for a comfy spot to sleep.

Who needs human children when you can get so much unconditional love from being owned by a cat?

RECEIVED 8/7

K.S.
Mission Viejo, CA

Cat Codependents often have a difficult time keeping the romance in their relationships.

People who love Cat Codependents often find themselves wondering "when will it be my turn?"

Dear Cat Codependents Anonymous,

I am 23 and everything I own has to do with cats. I currently have three cats.

My fiance has accepted his rank...#2 under my cats. He even tells others he knows where he ranks.

A.B.
Pulaski, VA

RECEIVED 4/5

Make no mistake, if you are courting a Cat Codependent, the cat's opinion of you is very important.

Dear Cat Codependents,

I am owned by Sir Lancelot (nickname "Lanci") who is a Bombay.

Lanci and I recently got rid of the husband, as he was a real pain. Therefore, one of my favorite sayings is "I got rid of the husband and kept the cat!" Lanci and I are a lot happier since we gave the husband the boot.

Purrs!

RECEIVED
1/6

D.R.
Lacey, WA

Never ask a Cat Codependent to choose between you and the cat.

Whenever a guy asks me out I ask him if he likes cats. If he says "no," I show him the door.

My mom has two cats, Penny and Mozart. She puts carpet out for them when they go sit in the snow so their bottoms don't get cold. We are definitely a cat codependent family. My mom asked me, "if your boyfriend didn't like cats, who would be the first to go?" Did she even have to ask?

D.M.
Aurora, CO

If you fall in love with a compulsive Cat Codependent, you better have plenty of bail money.

Those who care about Cat Codependents must help them to avoid situations which may be overpowering.

Virtually every Cat Codependent is susceptible to "love at first sight."

Sleep deprivation is the price Cat Codependents pay for their inability to say "no" to kitty.

Dear Cat Codependents,

I am a 19 year old college student. My family became cat codependent when I was in the 5th grade and my dad brought home Snowshoe, a stray. Now we have Missy and Frisky, (the late Snowshoe's grand kitties) as a vital part of our family. They make, and sometimes break, the rules. We often make sacrifices because Missy and Frisky get first choice of everything — the best chair, the best blanket, the best spot on the couch, and the majority of the bed.

But these are trivial sacrifices because there is nothing more upsetting than having your kitty mad at you!

I am forever devoted to my cats!

M.M.H.
Bossier City, LA

Chapter 4
Financial Consequences of Cat Codependency

Dear CatCo Anon;

Having been reared by cats from age 3 — my poor mother, God rest her soul, had long since given over care of me to the family cat after tripping over us both one too many times — I do believe I fill the requirements for being on your mailing list!

In my 66 years on this earth I have never willingly lived where my four legged family members were unwelcome. In more than one instance, it was "either my cats stay or we all go," resulting in house hunting expeditions until I came to the wise conclusion that it would be smarter to own my home than to rent...thus allowing me to have as many cats as it took to satisfy my soul.

Although my husband tried to retire 8 years ago, our 'owners' (our cats) told him in no uncertain terms that they would tolerate NO cutting back on anything for the sake of economy, and he was forced to take a part time job in order to support them in the manner to which they were accustomed. And now the poor man has been taken over by 2 more cats who have moved into the shop where he works and they also demand his attentions!

Please don't mistake me — we are both willing slaves to our masters, whom we love very much. But we need the aid of a support group to learn how to cope with this situation. Please! Put us on your mailing list right away! Thank you!

B.L.
La Grande, OR

Because Cat Codependents believe that it is their duty to feed every cat in the neighborhood, their food bills can be enormous.

Hi Cat Codependents Anonymous,

I have had cats in my home all my life. But about 4 years ago I fed a stray cat on the patio. He spread the word to all his feline pals and, to make a long story short, I now am caretaker of 40 (+) cats. I'm not really sure how many there are.

My husband built a kitty condo for them which we heat in the winter. The food bill is astronomical, but all they ask for is food and shelter and I get back love, affection, joy and the craziest antics when they perform. Anyone who has not experienced life with a cat has missed a love affair in its purest form.

L.L.
Warren, MI

Cat Codependents are often forced to pay top dollar for clothes that hide cat hair well.

Serious Cat Codependents learn to economize by buying in bulk.

Dear Cat Codependents,

I think I could truly count as a Cat Codependent. There are nine cats in my house at this time.

My husband and I started with one. We thought he would be lonely so we got him a cat companion. That was fine until we moved to a house. There were strays in the neighborhood. We have maintained a buffet on our enclosed back porch for the ensuing 6 1/2 years. There are seven gravity feed containers out there.

After my husband's death I took in another stray who turned out to be pregnant. I now have nine cats and I promise myself NO MORE, NINE IS ENOUGH!

I hope I can hold out.

Thanks,

M.T.
Chicago, IL

The holidays are particularly hard on a Cat Codependent's budget, since whatever kitty wants, kitty gets.

Dear Cat Codependents,

I admit it. I'm addicted to cats. I'm a little boy, eleven years old, and we own two male cats.

I am such a cat wacko that I celebrate their birthdays and buy them Christmas presents. They even have their own Christmas stockings.

Sonny, the younger cat, sleeps in my bed at night and I always give him a good night kiss...on the lips!

Each time I see a cat toy or catnip, I bother my Mom to buy it for them.

I hope I get better.

P.G.

RECEIVED 11/3

Cat codependent households often spend
more for veterinary services than they do
for rent.

My name is K-,

When we had to evacuate for hurricane Andrew I bought my cats an air
conditioned truck with a club cab so the seven of us could ride in harmony
and comfort. We were lucky. We had a home to return to.

The vet's office knows who I am when I phone. I pay the mortgage on their
building! I'm still single because I have six cats and can't get a date.

Thank you for maintaining my anonymity.

RECEIVED
5/19

K.Y.
Key Largo, FL

Many Cat Codependents find it necessary to work extra jobs to support their "cat habits."

Hi,

I feed every cat in the neighborhood. At this time I have spayed and neutered five cats. I have several more to go. I work a second job just to pay my vet and grocery bills (for cat food). I think I need to be on your mailing list.

Thanks,

K.R.
Fall River, MA

Cat Codependents often bring their problems to work with them, making it difficult for them to hold jobs.

Some Cat Codependents try to use their love of cats to support themselves. But because they form strong attachments to anything associated with their cats, this rarely proves profitable.

Dear Cat Codependent People,

Once I tried to raise and sell Persian cats. I played with the babies all day long. I loved them so much.

I advertised my babies for sale and when the day came to part with them I delivered them to the new owners. I cried my eyes into red balls. I cried for weeks.

I missed my babies so much that I begged to buy them back for more than I had been paid. I guess the new owners were cat codependent too because I wasn't able to get even one of them back.

I still raise Persians, but now I keep them all.

Yours,

J.B.
Mt. Vernon, WA

RECEIVED
7/3

Chapter 5
Cat Codependent Families

Dear Friends,

I recently bought the wonderful Cat Codependents Calendar in Fort Lauderdale, Florida, as a Christmas present for my Mother. Both my parents and I are great cat lovers. Our phone calls to one another often consist of more gossip about our cats than ourselves (after all, the cats have more free time to do noteworthy and interesting things). Our correspondence is always signed on behalf of all the household.

My Father takes his two cats, Ginger and Miss Brahms, on weekly trips to his beach house.

Unfortunately, my job on a cruise ship means that I am currently, unwillingly, 'between cats.' The golden days of ships having cats on board have (regrettably) gone along with sail and coal-powered vessels. I do try to compensate though by buying cat posters, postcards, sculptures, books, etc. from around the globe.

Furriest, purriest regards,

RECEIVED
12/3

L.K.
Auckland, New Zealand

Cat codependent families are easy to spot.

Cat codependent families take longer than most to count their blessings.

Dear Cat Co-Dependents Anonymous,

I started my own pet sitting service five years ago because of a suggestion from my husband. At that time we had only ten cats. I believe his theory was that if I could take care of many other peoples' cats we wouldn't be so susceptible to acquiring more of our own.

Needless to say, his "theory" went right down the tubes!!! We now have 21 cats, and number 22 is probably making his way up the drive as I write! The pet sitting service merely opened our lives up to an entire NETWORK of cats. Now, we don't simply care for others' animal companions (anyone with a leg in all four corners).

Do we spoil our babies? You bet we do! And no one is more deserving than our four legged family members.

K.M. O-M..
Lake Orion, MI

RECEIVED 2/16

Your first visit to a Cat Codependent
household can be a scary experience.

When you grow up in a cat codependent family,
you learn to endure many embarassments.

North Pole

If you have a cat codependent household,
everyone in town knows your address.

Wow!

I fit all of your symptoms of a Cat Codependent. Have you been watching
my house? This place looks like an orphanage. I really should be on T.V.
like Sally Struthers making an appeal for funds. My Mom brought me a
cat that she said she saw thrown from a truck; I've been trying to get
child support from her for 4 1/2 years. I need to be on your mailing list.

L.P.
Long Beach, CA

Many Cat Codependents think of their cats as surrogate children...

Dear Cat Codependents,

I am owned by Sasha. She is a beautiful Tonkinese. She enjoys watching Star Trek every night with her family in her very own chair. She did an impersonation of Data's cat Spot at a recent Star Trek convention that won the hearts of the entire audience.

Sasha has her own room and her own place at the dinner table. I share eating utensils with her and I always have a "Guess what Sasha learned to do" story.

In a lot of ways, she is my baby and I love her as if she were my own child.

S.S.
Tempe, AZ

…and they tend to be a little on the
overprotective side with their "kids."

In a cat codependent household, when kitty ain't happy, ain't nobody happy.

Dear Cat Codependents Anonymous,

I have a cat named Zucchini. He weighs 13.5 lbs and has a 13 inch tail which gets him into a lot of trouble. I have spent countless hours gluing things together after his tail has swept clean many a shelf.

My parents (from Iowa) nicknamed him "The Minnesota Monster." I wonder why? When I go home for a visit (Zucchi always comes with me) my Mother has to "cat proof" the house, move all the breakables, hide the dried flowers and clear the windowsills so Zucchi can perch on them to observe the squirrels and birds outside.

When friends pull out pictures of their children I pull out photos of Zucchi. When people talk about their family members I talk about Zucchi. Can I help it? Nope, I'm cat codependent.

K.A.M.
Rochester, MN

RECEIVED 3/2

Everyone in a cat codependent household must learn to perform the hairball manuever.

Chapter 6
Coping with Cat Codependence

(Note to the reader: You will, no doubt, notice the lack of
letters from Cat Codependents in this chapter. This is
because we don't get much mail from people who are
interested in becoming *less* dependent on their cats. R.S.)

Hi There,

Both my mother and I are Cat Codependents (we freely admit it, but we won't let our photos be published anywhere). Since Cat Codependents tend to hang together, I showed your calendar to all of my friends. We are relieved that someone has finally recognized our condition and is addressing it. Of course, none of us wants to be cured, you understand, but it's good to know that someone out there understands us.

I currently live with two cats. My boyfriend, who is not a cat person but is becoming numb to the presence of cats out of necessity, is suffering all the problems of one who becomes involved with a cat lover.

C.C.
Jackson, NJ

No evidence exists which offers hope for a cure for Cat Codependence. But with discipline, the condition can be managed. Unfortunately, millions of people either fail to realize that they have a cat problem, or choose to live in a state of denial.

Dear Cat Codependents,

I have recently become a Cat Codependent.

I did not realize that I had a problem until I received your calendar for Christmas. In looking over the calendar, and the letters from cat codependents in the back of the calendar, I saw the light. I cannot dispute or deny what I have become any longer.

Now I must learn to cope with my problem. I will face it with dignity and humor.

Thank you so much!

R.D.
Ft. Davis, TX

RECEIVED 10/4

Cat Codependents must learn to control their constant craving for affection or they will begin to alienate themselves from the very things they cherish the most.

Don't be fooled if a cat codependent tells
you she's on a "twelve step program."

At last I can admit it to someone who understands: I am a Cat
Codependent.

What's more, I have no will to overcome this all-consuming
affliction.

P.H.
San Antonio, TX

Support groups don't offer Cat Codependents much help either, as they almost always turn into cat shows.

Taking up a hobby can help to suppress a Cat Codependent's urge to acquire more cats.

Once you have admitted to yourself that you are a Cat Codependent, one of the first steps you must take to regain control of your life is to realize that there is a Higher Power and the Higher Power is not your cat!

If you are cat codependent, you must come to terms with the fact that you will always be cat codependent. Once you accept this you can move on to begin to regain your self esteem and live a more balanced life.

Use daily affirmations to keep yourself from backsliding.

Afterword

While everyone knows that Cat Codependence is a serious matter, the letters included in this book make it obvious that most Cat Codependents are comfortable — if not delighted — with their condition. If you are among them and don't have the slightest interest in controlling your cat codependency, then at least this book may help you to explain your feelings and behavior to family members, friends, and loved ones.

But if you are among the few who are ready to admit that their lives are out of control, then we hope this book will offer you help (and encouragement) as you learn to manage your condition.

Recovery is not a fast process. Take things one day at a time. Be sure to reward yourself for your successes along the way, no matter how small they might seem. Every pet store you walk past, every cat toy you leave on the shelf in the supermarket, every hour that you make it through without obsessing about your cat is a victory of the spirit. These victories need to be acknowledged, and as you pay tribute to yourself for your triumphs you will gradually become aware of your own power to make choices that are healthy and that leave you feeling good about yourself.

Most importantly, you must always remember that you are not alone. Millions, possibly even billions of people around the world are struggling with their cat codependency at this very moment.

If you are persistent enough, and if you can be compassionate with yourself, you will eventually regain control of your life. It may be the most difficult challenge you ever face, but rising up to meet the challenge will be worth it.

Those Cat Codependents who have faced the challenge and who stayed the course report that a change happened in their lives that they never anticipated: their relationships with their cats became better than it had ever been before.

As you and your cat slowly untangle your relationship, you will both become free to appreciate and love each other for who you really are without limiting or threatening each other's individuality and independence.

Nurtured by this new freedom and trust, your relationship will blossom and grow into something more wonderful than you ever imagined possible.

If you succeed, you must make sure you reward yourself with something *really* special . . . like a new kitten, for instance.

About the Author

Ronnie Sellers was born and raised in Philadelphia. He graduated from the University of Pennsylvania, where he was awarded the Phi Kappa Sigma Fellowship Award for prose.

He has written for radio, film and television and has authored three children's books, *If Christmas Were A Poem*, *When Springtime Comes* and *My First Day At School*.

In 1976 Ronnie was a co-founder of Renaissance Greeting Cards, where he created greeting cards for twelve years. In 1991 he formed his own publishing and licensing company, Ronnie Sellers Productions.

Ronnie has four children and lives and works in Kennebunk, ME.

About the Artist

Jennifer Black Reinhardt grew up in Hollidaysburg, PA and graduated from Carnegie Mellon University with a degree in Illustration. She is the creator of her own line of humorous greeting cards and was cited for her exceptional card design by the National Greeting Card Association in 1991.

Jennifer's work has been featured in several publications, including *The Artist's Market*, *The Best Contemporary Women's Humor*, and *The Complete Guide to Greeting Card Design and Illustration*.

She has recently written and illustrated her first children's book, *The Giant's Toybox*. She is also very happy to be illustrating *The Official Cat Codependents Calendar* and *The Official Dog Codependents Calendar*, both published by Ronnie Sellers Productions.